Edward Alexander Fry

The Registers of Beer Hackett, Dorset

1549 to 1812

Edward Alexander Fry

The Registers of Beer Hackett, Dorset
1549 to 1812

ISBN/EAN: 9783337144173

Printed in Europe, USA, Canada, Australia, Japan

Cover: Foto ©ninafisch / pixelio.de

More available books at **www.hansebooks.com**

The Registers

OF

Beer Hackett, Dorset.

FROM 1540 TO 1812.

TRANSCRIBED BY

EDWARD ALEXANDER FRY,

WITH THE PERMISSION OF

THE REV. WILFRED ROXBY, B.A.,
RECTOR OF THORNFORD AND BEER HACKETT.

LONDON:
PRIVATELY PRINTED FOR THE PARISH REGISTER
SOCIETY.

1896.

PREFACE.

The Registers of Beer Hacket, or Bere Hacket, to the year 1812 are contained in three volumes, the first of which commences in 1549. On the outside of the original cover of Vol. I is inscribed the following :—

"The Register Booke of the Parish of Berehackette "for Christenings, Wedings and burialls from the yeare of "our Lord God, 1549."

"Newelye written in the yeare of our Lord God "1600, Robert Pomerye and John Baulter being then "Churchwardens."

This Register as it now exists was made in accordance with the ordinance made in Convocation on the 25th October, 1597, which enjoined that the old registers on paper should be fairly and legibly written out into a parchment book. Vol. I measures 17¾ in. long by 8 in. wide, and is made of parchment, and contains 14 folios (28 pages). The entries are perfect from 1549 to 1630. Then follows three-quarters of a page containing entries for 1640, '41, '42, '46, '47, without, however, any apparent omissions. Then comes a break till 1658, from which date it is continuous to 1672, when there is another gap till 1696 ; from this date to 1707 it is perfect, then occurs a gap between 1707 to 1725, from which date to the end of the volume in 1745, it is perfect. In 1895 this volume was carefully mended and rebound.

Vol. II is likewise a parchment book, containing 56 pages, bound in whole calf, and measuring 12¼ in. by 7¾ in. Pages 1 to 3 contain Burials, 1773-1812. Pages 33 to 39 contain Baptisms, 1773-1812. Page 55 contains the dates on which the copies of the Register were sent up to the visitations held at Sherborne. Pages 4-32, 40-54 and 56 are blank.

The title of the book, written inside the cover, is:—

"Beer Hackett Register, in the County of Dorset, in
"the peculiar jurisdiction of the Dean of Sarum."

Vol. III is the usual folio book for Marriages from 1757 to 1812,
and contains 44 entries.

The following list of Patrons and Rectors is taken from Hutchin's
"History of Dorset," Vol. IV, page 120, with some additions by Rev.
Canon Mayo:—

PATRONS.	RECTORS.
———	Thomas Freeman exchanged with
—— ——	Robert Eye (or Yli or Yke) rector or Hasilbury Brian, instituted to the rectory of the *capella curata* of Bere Hacket, in the jurisdiction of the Abbot of Sherborne, 4 Aug., 1397, exchanged with
Silvester Everard.	Stephen Frogmere, Rector of Lazarton (anciently a distinct parish, but united in 1431 with Stour Payne), instit. 16 Dec., 1399. He occurs in Dean Chandler's Register in 1405.
-———	Nicholas Shudde, 1408.
———	Amias Himyngame, buried 30 Dec., 1549.
Thomas Downton.	Henry Smith, instit. 1549, buried 24 May, 1561.
———	William Andrews, died 1576.
———	John Downton, instit. 22 March, 1576, buried — Jan., 1625.
———	Richard Jefferyes, instit. 1625.
———	Henry Browne, instit. 1636.
—— -	Hugh Strode, instit. 1637, sequestered by the Parliamentary Committee.
———	*Thomas Browne*, intruder, officiated 1649 and subsequently.
—— -	**James Pope*, 1650, also an intruder.
John Strode.	*Francis Murrall*, presented 5 July, 1658, on cession of the last incumbent (Lambeth, MSS., No. 1587).

The return of "The Commission to inquire of Church Livings in the County of
Dorset, 13 Die Novembris, 1650," is thus worded:—"Beer Hackwood (*sic*). Wee
have one parsonage and one Prebend. The Parsonage worth £40 p. annum and
the Prebend worth £10. Mr. Pope, a preaching Minister, supplies the Cure and
hath the profit of the Parsonage and the Earl of Bristow hath the Prebend. Wee
have a very fitt Church conveniently scituated. We have noe Chappels to be
united or taken away. Wee have no need of a New Church to be built or our Parish
divided.

PATRONS.	RECTORS.
John Strode.	John Duncomb, instit. 15 Jan., 1662, died 1690.
ditto	Haynes Ryal (or Royal), B.A. (son of Henry Ryall [or Royall] of Sherborne) Wadham Coll., Oxford, matric. 21 Mch. 1683-4, æt. 17, B.A. 19 Mch., 1687-8. Instit. 1 July, 1690, Also Rector of Thornford, buried there 28 May, 1702.
Ann Lewys.	Henry Emery* or Embris, (son of Richard Emery or Embris of Blandford), Wadham Coll., Oxford, matric. 17 Dec., 1685, æt. 18 B.A. from New Inn Hall, 13 Mch., 1689-90. Instit. 15 May, 1703. Also Rector of Thornford, died —— 1743.
———	Robert Sampson (son of Robert Sampson of Sherborne), Queen's Coll., Oxford, matric. 20 March, 1731-2, æt. 18, B.A. 1735. Instit. 1743. Also Rector of Thornford, buried there 1770.
———	Robert Sampson, son of preceding, Pembroke Coll., Oxford, matric. 15 Mch., 1762, æt. 17, B.A. 1766.
John Munden.	John Munden, LL.D. (son of John Munden of Bere Hacket). Rector and Lord of the Manor, 1786. He was also Rector of Corscombe in this country. Died 1821, and buried at Bere Hacket.
Sir John Munden, and W. Helyar, Esq.	Hugh Welman Helyar, M.A., St. John's Coll., Cambridge, instit. 1825 (?) Also Rector of Sutton Bingham, co. Som.
———	Arthur Chichester Burnard, B.A., Brazenose Coll., Oxford, instit. 1877, resig. 1883.
Rev. A. C. Burnard.	Robert James Duncan, M.A., Wadham Coll., Oxford, instit. 1883. Died 7 Nov., 1891, aged 42. Buried at Bere Hacket. Was Rector of Grosmont, co. Mon., 1874-1882.
Robert Duncan, Esq.	Wilfred Roxby, B.A., Emmanuel Coll., Cambridge, instit. 5 March, 1892. Also Rector of Thornford.

EDWARD ALEXANDER FRY.

* Previous to Jan., 1731-2, he signs the Register as Henry Emery, but after this date as Henry Embris.

Beere Hackette.

The Register Booke of the names of them that shalbe Christened Married and buried w'th the dayes of their christeninge marryinge and buryinge made the Eight Day of August in the yeare of our Lord God 1549 in the Second yeare of the Reigne of Edward the Sixth Kinge of England France and Ireland defender of the Fayth etc.

And Now in the Year 1600 and in the yeare of the Reigne of our Sov'aign Ladie Queen Elizabeth by the grace of God of England France and Ireland Queen, defender of the fayth, the 42 trulie taken out of the paper Register Booke by **John Downton** person of the psh aforesaid as followeth; But first noate that the yeare of our Lord God of this Register booke begineth the XXVth daye of March.

1549.

Robert Bavller the sonne of John Bavller was baptized 8 August.

John Stooke and Alic Dalye the daughter of John Dallye were married 7 September.

Walter Dowle the sonne of Willm Dowle was baptised 10 October.

Amyas Binnygame p'sone of this church was burried 30 December.

William Panter the sonne of Hugh Panter was baptised 19 January.

John Newman the sonne of Willm Newman was baptised 20 February.

Marye Churchouse the daughter of John Churchouse was baptised 29 Feb.

1550.

John Hawkings was buried 16 Maye.

1551.

Edward Dowle the sonne of Willm Dowle was baptised 5 June.

James Rawsonne was baptised 12 July.

William Rawsonne was buryed 25 October.

William Bavller the sonne of John Bavller the younger was baptised 5 February.

(Signature at foot of page) Amyas Hinningame.
Henry Smithe.

1

1552.

Richard Chaplin was maryed (*sic*) 3 Aprill.
Hugh Panter the sonne of Hugh Panter was baptised 29 June.
Edward Harrys and Anne Churchouse were maryed 17 July.
Thomas Newman the sonne of Walter Newman was buryed 10 August.
Tobyas Dowle the sonne of Willm̄ Dowle was baptised 20 Aug.
Bridget the daughter of John Churchouse was baptised 17 December.
Thomas Newman the sonne of Willm̄ Newman was baptised 15 January.
I. pott was maryed to Margret Rawsonnes 28 Jan.

1553.

Thomas Master was maryed to Edith Smynns (*sic*) 8 Maye.
Katherin Potte was baptised 7 January.
Joan Bavller the daughter of John Bavller was baptised 10 March.

1554.

Alexander Dowle the sonne of William Dowle was baptised 14 February.

1555.

Anne Panter the daughter of Hugh Panter was baptised 19 Aprill.
Edeth Newman the daughter of William Newman was baptised 14 Julye.
Alice Harris was baptised 17 August.
Thomas ——— was baptised 30 February (*sic*).
William Bavller was buryed 4 March.

1556.

Johan Master was baptised 1 April.
Margaret Panter the daughter of Hugh Panter was baptised 20 Julye.
Walter Churchouse the sonne of John Churchouse was baptised 5
    December.
William Newman the sonne of Willm. Newman was baptised 3 January.
Edward Lambert the son of Thomas Lambert was baptised 13 February.

1557.

John Newman thelder was buryed 20 Maye.
Katherin Panter was buryed 12 December.

(Signature at foot) Henry Smithe.

Page 3.   Original paging 2.

John Tayler was buryed 13 December.
John Masters was buryed 16 Dec.

1558.

Johan Newman was buryed 12 June.
Agnes Bauller the daughter of John Bauller was baptis. 19 Julye.
Richard Master was baptised 8 October.

1559.

Katherin Pomerye the daughter of Robte Pomerye was baptised 4
    September.

1560.

Christopher Moore and Margrett Dowle was maryed 20 November.
Thomas Bauller the sonne of John Bauller was baptised 24 Februarie.
Edeth Bauller the daughter of John Bawller was baptised idem.

1561.

Ibcnric Smitbe p'sonn of this pish was buried 24 Maye.
William Moore the sonne of Christopher Moore was baptised 9 June.
Henry Newman the sonne of Willñ Newman was baptised 26 June.
Elizabeth Rawsomes was buryed 28 June.
Thomas Bauller the sonn of John Bauller was buryed 6 September.

1562.

Raulfe Potkine and Allis Harris ware maryed 2 November.
George Harris the sonne of Edward Harris was baptised 7 February.

1563.

Margarett Lambert the daughter of Thomas Lambert was baptised
  3 June.
Dorathye Rawsome the daughter of Richard Rawsome was baptised
  22 June.
Bennet Bauller the sonne of John Bauller was baptised 4 September.
William Dowle was buryed 10 November.
John Latchmore and Margarett Newman were maryed 21 January.
Joane servante of Thomas Dowle was buryed 12 March.

1564.

Samuell Pomery the sonne of Robert Pomery was baptised 5 June.
(Signatures at foot) Henry Smithe.
William Androwes.

Page 4.
Elizabeth Master the wyfe of Willñ Master was buryed 21 November.
Joane Hannam and John her sonne were buryed 14 January.
Edward Moore the sonne of Christopher Moore was baptised 18
  February.
Isable Lambert was baptised 27 Feb.

1565.

John Newman the sonne of William Newman was baptised 16 April.
John Bauller the sonne of John Bauller was baptised 29 November.
John Pomerye the sonne of Robert Pomerye was baptised 23 Februarie.

1566.

Margerye Moore the daughter of Xpofer Moore was baptised 25 January.

1567.

Joane daughter of Robert Dowle was baptised 18 Aprill.

1568.

John Newman the sonne of Willñ Newman was baptised 29 Aprill.
Margery Master the daughter of William Master was baptised 15 July.

1569.

Thomas Masson was baptised 10 October.
John Keytt and Dorothy Newman were maried 16 Oct.
Richard Moore the sonne of Xpofer Moore was baptised 8 Februarie.

1570.

Elinour Keate the daughter of John Keate was baptised 28 June.
Richard Moore was buried 27 August.
Eme Dowle the daughter of Robte Dowle was baptised 20 September.
Allis Dowle was buryed 15 December.
Margery Master the daughter of Willñ Master was baptised 19 Dec.
Margarett Master was buryed 5 January.

1571.

Philipp Kymppe was buried 20 July.
John Moore the sonne of Christopher Moore was baptised 31 October.
Thomas and John the sonnes of Willñ Master was (*sic*) baptised 30 December.
John Masters buryed 1 January.
Thomas Masters buryed 2 January.

1572.

Agnis Kimpe was buryed 30 November.
Ellinor Masters the daughter of Willm Masters was baptised 2 March

(Signature at foot) William Androwes.

Page 5.   Original paging 3.

1573.

Joane Keate the daughter of John Keate was baptised 1 April.
Ideth Write the daughter of Roger Wiite was baptised 30 June.
Idith Gibbs the daughter of John Gibbs was baptised 28 February.

1574.

Phillip Keate the sonne of John Keate was baptised 4 September.
Peeter Clench and Margaret Thorne were maryed 17 October.
Dorethye Pomery the daughter of Robert Pomery was baptised 19 November.

1575.

John Moore the sonne of Christopher Moore was buryed 30 (*sic*) February.

1576.

Richard Wright the sonne of Roger Wright was baptised 3 June.
Thomas Master the sonne of Willñ Master was baptised 8 August
☞ **William Androwes** pson of this Church was buryed at Yetminster 5 October.
Joane Newman was buryed 18 Oct.

1577.

Bridget Gibbs the daughter of John Gibbs was baptised 30 May.
John Keate the sonne of John Keate was baptised 20 October.

Edward Whittell and Bridget Churchouse were maryed 28 November.
Joane Dowle was buryed 14 Nov.
James Morrys and Elinor Lambert were maryed 24 January.

1578.
John Ingelbert was buryed 16 August.

1579.
William Wright the sonne of Roger Wright was baptised 5 January.
Margery Miller the daughter of John Miller was baptised 14 Jan.
Em Keate the daughter of John Keate was baptised 20 February.

1580.
Joane Masters the daughter of William Masters was baptised 7 May.
Thomas Dowle was buryed 12 May.
Robert Pomery the sonne of Robert Pomery was baptised 8 June.

(Signatures at foot of page) William Androwes.
John Downton.

Page 6.
John Churchouse was buryed 4 November.
Elizabeth Masters was buryed 23 November.

1581.
William Moore was buryed 23 May.
John Miller the sonn of Peeter Miller was baptised 26 September.
Robert Saunders and Joane Lambert were married 13 October.
Hugh Panter was buryed 6 January.
Lionell Miller the sonne of John Miller was baptised 1 February.

1582.
Richard Keate the sonne of John Keate was baptised 7 Aprill.
John Jeanes the sonne of Richard Jeanes was baptised 29 Julye.
Dorathie Gibbs the daughter of John Gibbs was baptised 30 July.

1583.
Richard Joyce the sonne of William Joyce was baptised 7 Aprill.
Elizabeth Master was baptised 15 Aprill.
Thomas Stounte was buryed 18 December.

1584.
Edward Thomas the sonne of John Thomas was baptised 2 Maye.
Richard Waters and Joane Pomery were maried 18 Maye.
Margaret Panter the daughter of Hugh Panter was baptised 23 August.
Em Churchouse the daughter of John Churchouse was baptised 31 December.
Henry Keat the sonne of John Keate was baptised 22 January.
John Gibbs the sonne of John Gibbs was baptised 13 March.

1585.
Joane Smith was buried 23 May.
Thomas Bonfield and Ideth Newman were maried 6 June.

Henry Keate was buryed 8 June.
Margaret Watters was baptised 12 June.
Dorathie Panter was baptised 26 January.

1586.

Elizabeth Bauller was buryed 20 December.

1587.

Emme Farre the daughter of Henry Farre was baptised 29 October.
Able Churchouse the sonne of Robert Churchouse was baptised 30 November.
Margarett Cole the daughter of Andrew Cole was baptised 14 December.

(Signature at foot) John Downton.

Page 7.   Original paging 4.

John Clench was buryed 21 January.
John Newman was buryed 6 February.
Elizabeth Panter the daughter of Hugh Panter was baptisid 25 Feb.
Edward Waters the sonne of Richard Waters was baptised 24 March.

1588.

Samuell Pomery and Emme Barnard were maryed 3 November.
Anthony Hodges and Margaret Lambert,
Richard Bearlye and Margaret Panter were maried } 4 Nov.

1589.

Margaret Gibbs was baptised 12 September.
Robert Pomery was baptised 14 Sept.
Allis Churchouse the daughter of Robert Churchouse was baptised 24 Dec.
Margery Pomery was baptised 11 January.

1590.

Emme Miller the daughter of John Miller was baptised 24 May.
Agnes Chappell was buryed 24 March.

1591.

Allis Hill was buryed 19 Aprill.
Thomas Lambert was buryed 17 May,

1592.

John Miller was buryed 20 May.
Grace Panter the daughter of Hugh Panter was baptised 24 May.
Thomas Pomery was baptised 23 Aprill (*sic*).

1593.

William Rowswell the sonne of Thomas Rowswell was baptised 24 April.
Ellin Turke was buryed 10 May.
Joane Newman the daughter of Thomas Newman was baptised 26 December.
John Cobbe the sonne of Willm Cobbe was baptised the 3 March.

1594.

Allis Newman the daughter of Henry Newman was baptised 14 July.

1595.

Mary Bauller the daughter of John Bauller was baptised 5 October.
Thomas Dowle and Ellinor Master were maryed 9 January.

1596.

Hugh Panter the sonne of Hugh Panter was baptised 2 May.
Lyonell Turke and Margaret Churchouse were maryed 9 May.
John Gibbes was buryed 2 February.

(Signature at foot) John Dowaton.

Page 8.

1596.

*Joane Panter was buryed.

1597.

*Richard Dowle the sonne of Thomas Dowle was baptised.
*Richard Bauller the sonne of Bennett Bauller was baptised.
*Ellinor Gibbs the daughter of Robert Gibbs was baptised.

1598.

*Martha Bauller the daughter of John Bauller was baptised.
*Lyonell Turke the sonne of Lyonell Turke was baptised.
*John Bauller was buryed.
*Idith Pannter the daughter of Hugh Panter was baptised.
*Joane Churchouse was buryed.
*Ursula Newman the daughter of Henry Newman was baptised.

1599.

*James Lester and Margaret Clench were maryed.
*William Miller and Margaret Speed were maryed.
*Joane Pomery the daughter of Samuel Pomery was baptised.
Edward Moore the sonne of Edward Moore was baptised 15 July.
Christian Churchouse the daughter of Robert Churchouse was baptised 1 August.
Grace Gibbs the daughter of Robert Gibbs was baptised 4 January.
Emme Bauller the daughter of Bennett Bauller was baptised 6 January.
Margery Newman the daughter of Thomas Newman was baptised 17 February.
Joane Lodge was buryed 3 March.

1600.

Thomas Turke the sonne of Lyonell Turke was baptised 16 Maye.
Anne Bauller the daughter of John Bauller was baptised 20 July.
Dorathie Dowle the daughter of Thomas Dowle was baptised 24 August.
Dorathie Churchouse was buried 12 September.

---

*A strip about 10 inches long having been cut out of the right hand side of the page, the days of the month cannot be given.

1601.

Emme Newman the daughter of Henrie Newman was baptised 29 March.

William Masters was buried 6 June.

George Harris the sonne of George Harris was baptised 20 December.

Alice Bauler was buried 18 Januarie.

(Signature at foot) John Downton.

Page 9.   Original paging 5.

John Gibbs the son of Bridgett Gibbs was baptised 28 February.

Ursula Gibbs the daughter of Robert Gibbs was baptised 21 March.

John Churchouse the sonne of Robert Churchouse was baptised 24 March.

1602.

John Kinge was buried 10 April.

Joane Pomery was buried 12 April.

Elinor Bauler the daughter of Benett Bauler was baptised 6 June.

Elinor Pomery the daughter of Robert Pomery was baptised 29 September.

Robert Panther the sonne of Hugh Panther was baptised 28 Oct.

Anne Turke the daughter of Lionell Turke was baptised 12 December.

Grace Hull the daughter of Thomas Hull was baptised 26 December.

William Newman was buried 29 December.

1603.

Grace Bauler the daughter of John Bauler was baptised 26 April.

James Masters the sonne of John Masters was baptised 15 May.

Henry Masters the sonne of Thomas Masters was baptised 27 November.

John Collins the sonne of John Collins was baptised 4 (month illegible).

1604.

William Harris the sonne of George Harris was baptised 25 June.

Susan Newman the daughter of Henry Newman was baptised 9 September.

Joane Pomery the daughter of Robert Pomery was baptised 16 September.

Christian Bauler the daughter of Benett Bauler was baptised 25 November.

1605.

John Strode the sonne of William Strode was baptised 29 March.

Alice Turke the daughter of Lionell Turke was baptised 21 May.

William Traske and Alice Churchouse were married 15 Sept.

George Gibbs the sonne of Robert Gibbs was baptised 8 Dec.

John Bauler the sonne of John Bauler was baptised 16 February.

(Signature at foot) John Downton.

Page 10.

Susan Dowle the daughter of Thomas Dowle was baptised 2 March.

1606.

Roger Gregorie and Jane Masters were married 21 June.
Thomas Cleeves and Elizabeth Masters were married 22 June.
Joane Lodge was buried 29 June.
John Traske the sonne of William Traske was baptised 13 July.
Elinor Newman was buried 17 October.
Phillipp Turke was buried 27 October.
Scipio Stuclie the sonne of Scipio Stuclie was baptised 2 November.
John Pomery the sonne of Robert Pomery was baptised 8 March.

1607.

Ann Newman the daughter of Henry Newman was baptised 7 April.
Magdalen Masters the daughter of John Masters was baptised 22 November.
Alice Newman the daughter of Thomas Newman was baptised 27 December.
Robert Pomery was buried 28 December
Joane Wadlowe was buried 29 December.
Ann Turke was buried 8 January.
Lionell Turke was buried 15 January.
Emme Turke the daughter of Lionel Turke was baptised 3 March.

1608.

William Bauler the sonne of John Bauler was baptised 17 April.
Elizabeth Dowle the daughter of Thomas Dowle was baptised 9 October.
George Pomery the sonne of Robert Pomery was baptised 22 January.
Henry Traske the sonne of William Traske was baptised 8 February.

1609.

Joane Harrison the daughter of Lionell Harrison was baptised 17 April.
Robert Bauler was buried 8 June.
John Masters the sonne of Thomas Masters was baptised 20 August.
Joane Chamberlayne was buried 1 February.

(Signature at foot) John Downton.

Page 11.   Original paging 6.

Lewes Harris the sonne of Edward Harris was baptised 18 February.

1610.

Marie Newman the daughter of Henry Newman was baptised 18 Aprill.
John Masters was buried 14 May.
Jane Farr was buried 18 May.
Joane Newman was buried 5 September.
Alice Pomery was buried 8 September.
Michael Dewey and Margarett Pomery were married 22 October.
Thomas Churchouse was buried 7 December.
Walter Shane and Elinor Gillome were married 3 February.
Basill Bauler the daughter of Bennett Bauler was baptised idem.
Robert Churchouse the sonne of Abell Churchouse was baptised 17 March.

1611.

Thomas Masters the sonne of Thomas Masters was baptised 1 April.
*Hugh Wolmington and Emme Farr were married 4 Nov.
Elinor Newman the daughter of Henry Newman was baptised 11 Dec
Emme Downton was buried 23 Dec.
Robert Pomery the sonne of Robert Pomery was baptised 20 Feb.

1612.

Joane Bauler the daughter of John Bauler was baptised 23 April.
Thomas Dowle the sonne of Thomas Dowle was baptised 5 July.
Bridgett Thomas the daughter of John Thomas was baptised 6 August.
Walter Mows and Margerie Devoll were married 2 (?) Sept.
Henry Woolmenton the sonne of Hugh Woolmenton was baptised
    17 January.

1613.

Margerie Lamberte was buried 25 March.
Samuel Masters the sonne of Thomas Masters was baptised 19 Aprill.
John Panther the sonne of Margarett Panther was baptised 29 April.
Walter Shane the sonne of Walter Shane was baptised 13 June.
Martha Churchouse the daughter of Abell Churchouse was baptised
    20 June.

(Signature at foot) John Downton.

Page 12.

Samuell Pomery the sonne of Robert Pomery was baptised 9 January.
Margarett Newman the daughter of Henry Newman was baptised
    1 February.

1614.

Dorathie Woollmenton the daughter of Hugh Woollmenton was baptised
    7 August.
William Dowle the sonne of Thomas Dowle was baptised 8 January.
Richard Chedde and Alice Harris were married 30 January.
Elizabeth Bauler the daughter of John Bauler was baptised 12 March.

1615.

Ralph Guye and Margarett Turke were married 16 October.
Elinor Masters the daughter of
    Thomas Masters was baptised 3 February.

1616.

Thomas Pomery the sonne of Roberte Pomery was baptised 31 March.
George Churchouse the sonne of Richard Churchouse was baptised
    3 Aprill.
William Bauler was buried 30 Aprill.
Martin Snell was buried 7 June.

---

*This entry is in the margin.

Joane Webber was buried 23 October.
Emme Woollmenton the daughter of Hugh Woollmenton was baptised
 3 November.
Henry Churchouse the sonne of Abell Churchouse was baptised
 2 January.
Richard Chedde the sonne of Richard Chedde was baptised 22 January.

1617.

Edmonnde Yeate and Elinor Newman were married 22 September.
Lionell Churchouse the sonne of Richard Churchouse was baptised
 29 September.
John Lye was buried 22 October.
Robert Masters the sonne of Thomas Masters was baptised 11 January.
Elizabeth Snell was buried 12 January.

1618.

Peter Thomas the sonne of John Thomas was baptised 12 Aprill.
William Churchouse the sonne of William Churchouse was baptised
 (no date given).
(Signature at foot) John Downton.

Page 13.   Original paging 7.

Henry Browne and Ann Bauler were married 9 June.
William Newman the sonne of Henry Newman was baptised 13 Sep-
 tember.
Richard Webber the sonne of John Webber was baptised 22 November.
Samuell Pomery and Joane Sumer were married 27 January.
Thomas Churchouse the sonne of Richard Churchouse was baptised
 2 February.

1619.

Elizabeth Churchouse the daughter of William Churchouse was baptised
 2 May.
Joane Browne the daughter of Henry Browne was baptised 30 May.
Dorathie Masters was buried (no date given).
Robert Watts and Ann Lamberte were married 19 October.
George Masters and Martha Bauler were married 28 November.
Grace Churchouse the daughter of William Churchouse was baptised
 1 January.
Hester Masters the daughter of Thomas Masters was baptised 13
 February.
Thomas Kente the sonne of Symon Kente was baptised 20 February.
Agnes Dowle the daughter of Thomas Dowle was baptised (torn)
 February.
Marie Webber the daughter of John Webber was baptised 26 February.

1620.

Nathaniell Downton the sonne of John Downton was baptised (torn)
 Aprill.
James Churchouse the sonne of Richard Churchouse was baptised (torn).

Joane Browne was buried 17 September.
Joane Hutchings the daughter of Jesper Hutchings was baptised
   1 October.
George Write and Grace Hull were married 3 December.
Thomas Watts the sonne of Robert Watts was baptised 28 January.
Grace Masters the daughter of George Masters was baptised 28 January.
         (Signature at foot) John Downton.
     Page 14.

1621.

Ann Bauler was buried 27 Aprill.
Joane Churchouse the daughter of William Churchouse was baptised
   24 June.
Thomas Hodges *otherwise* Poore and Christian Churchouse were married
   18 October.
Richard Luckis the sonne of William Luckis was baptised 1 November.
Margarett Write the daughter of George Write was baptised 8 December.
Beñett Bauler was buried 1 January.
John Webber the sonne of John Webber was baptised 3 March.

1622.

Katherine Churchouse the daughter of Able (*sic*) Churchouse was
   baptised 6 Aprill.
Thomas Hodges *otherwise* Poore the sonne of Thomas Hodges *other-*
   wise Poore was baptised 14 Aprill.
James Lodge was buried 20 Aprill.
Thomas Kente was buried 24 May.
Alice Newman the daughter of Henrie Newman was baptised 23 June.
Margaret Browne the daughter of Henry Browne was baptised 4 August.
Thomas Juxon and Katherine Waldron were married 6 September.
Mary Hutchings the daughter of Jesper Hutchings was baptised
   15 November.
Alice Newman was buried 25 December.
Henry Newman was buried 30 December.
Alice Newman was buried 12 Januarie.
James Goldringe and Emm Panter were married 10 March.

1623.

Agnes Churchouse the daughter of William Churchouse was baptised
   6 Aprill.
Agnes Snell was buried 13 June.
George Masters the sonne of George Masters was baptised 22 June.
Agnes Churchuse (*sic*) was buried 9 September.
Ideth Churchowse the daughter of Richard Churchowse was baptised
   26 October.
        (Signature at foot) John Downton.
    Page 15.   Original paging 8.
Anne Golderinge the daughter of James Golderinge was baptised 28
   October.

Jerman Write the sonne of George Write was baptised 2 November.
John Snell and Mary Coventrye were maried 26 January.
*Christian Churchowse was buried 25 March.

1624.

Ertha (*sic*) Luckis the sone of William Luckis was baptised 4 April.
Lionell Browne was buried 29 May.
Jane Wolmington the daughter of Hugh Wolmington was baptised 15 August.
Elizabeth Pommery daughter of Samuel Pomery was baptised 6 October.
☞ John Downton parson of Beerhackett and Joan Symes *als* Ford were married 7 Apprill.
Alexander Bartlet and Susanah Hulett were married 24 May.
Francis Mast and Katherine Ginre were maried 28 October.
John Churchouse the sone of William Churchouse was bap. 5 November.
Jerman Write was buried 29 January.
Susana Goldring the daughter of James Goldring was baptised 16 February.
Robert Master the sone of Francis Masters was bap. 19 March.
Roger Churchouse the sone of Abell Churchouse was bap. 20 March.

1625.

John Hatkins the son of John Hatkins was bap. — April.
Constance Webber the daughter of John Webber was bap. 1 May.
Edward Lambert and Eliner Pommery were married the 23 May.
Mary Masters the daughter of Georg Masters was bap. (date torn away).
Anne Write the daughter of Georg Write was bap. (date torn away.)
☞ John Downton Parson was buried Jan.† (date torn away).
George Gibbes and Margarett (name almost illegible ? if Lacy) were maryed 8 January.
Anne Larnbeth (*sic*) the daughter of Edward Lamberd (*sic*) was bap. 12 February.
Joane Burt was buried 28 February.
Joan Luckis the daughter of Willm Luckis was bap. 5 March.

1626.

Joane Hutchins was buried 26 March.
Anne the daughter of Robert Woolcott, clerk was bap. 22 May.
Valentine Farding was buried 6 June.
Robert Burt and Emme Newman were maried 30 June.

(Signatures at foot) John Downton.
　　　　　　　　　　　Nicholaus Jeffris.

---

*To this point the writing is of one uniform character.

† Jan. with a stroke through it appears in the body of the page, but the margin here is torn away.

Page 16.

James Goldring the sonne of Francis Goldring was bap. 29 November.
Jane Masters the daughter of Francis Masters bap. 24 November (*sic.*)

1627.

Henry Churchowse the sonne of William Churchowse was baptised
26 May.
Mary Churchowse the daughter of Abell Churchowse was baptised
10 July.
Margarett Gibbes was buried 10 August.
John Gibbes the sonne of George Gibbes was baptised 11 August.
Anne Pomery the daughter of Samuell Pomery was baptised 8
September.
Joseph Birte the sonne of Robert Birte was baptised 27 December.
Johane Lambert the daughter of Edward Lambert was baptised 6
Januari.
Katharine Raynoldes *alias* Farr the daughter of Richard Farr *alias*
Raynoldes was baptised 13 Januari.
William Master the sonne of George Master was baptised 13 Januari.
Hanna Hatkins the daughter of John Hatkins was baptised 11
Februari.
Katharine Wolmyngton the daughter of Hugh Wolmyngton was baptised
19 Februari.

1628.

Henry Churchowse was buried 11 Maye.
Alice Farr was buried 28 Maye.
George Gibbes and Dorathy Dowle were married 18 August.
Eideth Hull was buried 29 October.
John Master the sonne of Francis Master was baptised 19 November.
Sara Riall the daughter of Richard Riall was baptised 20 December.
John Luckis the sonne of William Luckis was baptised 25 January.
William Brame [or Braine] and Grace Bauller were married 2 February.

1629.

Roger Goldringe the sonne of James Goldringe was baptised 29 March.

1630.

John Bauler was buried 6 Aprill.
Eliner Lambert the daughter of Edward Lambert was baptised 26
Aprill.
Joseph Webber and Beniamin Webber the sonnes of John Webber
were baptised 20 June.
Joseph Webber was buried 20 June.
Beniamin Webber was buried 29 July.

(Signature at foot) Nicholaus Jeffris. R.

The yeare of our Lorde 1640, and in the 16th of King Charles.

1640.

† Samuel Masters married Julian ————, 29 Jun.

Joseph Pomery the sone of Samuel Pomery was baptised 13 September.

Grace Churche house was buried 20 September.

Robert Panter the sone of Robert Panter was baptised 20 October.

John Lambard was buried 8 September.

Abell Church house was buried 6 January.

Joan Masters was buried 17 January.

John Riall the son of Richard Riall was baptised 19 January.

Ceusan Gouldring was buried 9 Feb.

1641.

Gregorye Pond and Julian Millet of Sherborne were married 20 July.

Peter (?) Newman ye sone of William Newman was baptised 27 July.

Richard Harris was buried 26 Dec.

‡ 1642.

Jane Master the daughter of George Master was baptised 26 Oct.

‡ 1646.

The same day was buried Jane Churchhowse daughter of Robert Churchowse 8 June.

William Pomery the son of Samuell Pomery was baptised 14 June.

William Bawller the sonne of William Bawller was baptised 22 September.

Thomas Pinker the son of Thomas Pinker was baptised 26 September.

[Henceforward in another hand.]

John Allwod the sonn of John Allwod and Margaret Allwod his wife was baptised 2 Februarie.

James Allwood was baptised (no date).

— Yeare of our Lord God 1647 and 17th of Kinge Charles.

Page 18. Page 18 is blank, but is headed

Berehacket Aᵒ Donni 1648.

---

* Pages 17 and 18 are three-quarters only of a whole sheet. It was found loose in the parish chest, one of several that evidently are now lost or destroyed, for there are many hiati from hence forward.

† This is in a later hand.

‡ There were, apparently, no entries between 26 October, 1642, and 8 June, 1646.

Page 19.   Original paging 12.

* The marige (?) of Robert Foarde and Elesabeth Addams, bride, Loaders on Thursday July fourth day in ye year Anno Dni 1695 at Thornford.
* Mr. Elnar Mintern of Yeatminster Elezabeth Hearn widow of Bemester, his bride, Loaders.
* John Mintern jun of Yeatminster.
* John Munden jun (*sic*) of Bearhackett his bride Loaders writen per me Robertus Foarde gent.

The year of our Lord God 1658 and ——— year of King ———.
(Torn) the daughter of John Lokier of Sock widdow (?) of William Newman of Knighton deceased and was buried ye same day at Beare Hagget.
* Robert Foarde borne Tuesday at 4 a clock in morning November 21st day in ye yeare Anno Dni 1676 in ye town of Beamester.

[1658]

Richard Gwyer of Leigh was buried — Nov.
* Robert Foarde sin. died Tuesday 4 at clock in morning 7th day of May 1688 in Beamester.
* Robert Foarde sin burried Fryday May 10th Ano 1688 in Beamester.

The year of our Lord God 1688 and —— — year of King ——— —
* The above written Robert Foarde sen dyed in ye 49th year of his age on ye 7th of May in 1688 witnes his son Robertus Foarde.

1659.

Ellen Gwyer was buried 28 Aprill.
Susanna the daughter of Edward and Charitye Harris was baptised and was born the 20th of April 31 May.

Page 20.

1659.

3 Jan Being Tuesday about 9 of ye clocke at night departed this life Mrs Constance Guppey, widdowe, aged 80 yeares. She was the daughter of Thomas Kingsmell of Kings Eenham in the Countye of Southampton, Esq, sister to Sr John Kingsmill of Wallingtons in the Countye of Berkeshire Knight. Relict of Richard Guppey of Sandridgehill Parke in the Countye of Wiltshire, gent. And Mother to Constance the wife of John Strode of Knighton or Ryme, gent.
9 Jan. The said Constance was buried in the Chancell of the parish Church of Yeatminster.

---

* The entries in the execrable writing of Robert Forde, jun., marked with an asterisk, are made in blank spaces that happened to exist on pages 20 and 21, for they are of a much later date than the few other entries which are in their proper places on these pages.

— Feb.   Margaret Panter spinster was buried.
— March.   Hugh Panter her brother was also buried.

The yeare of our Lord God 1660 the twelveth yeare of the reign of [torn] Lord King Charles the Second.

1660.

— June.   Elizabeth the daughter of William Master [torn].
8 July.   William Newman of Knighton [torn].
15   „   Grace ye wife of George Write of [torn].
*21 April.   Susanna Gooldring was baptised.
*6 Oct.   Edward son of Edw. Harris bapt.

Edward Noake his hand and pen.

† The same Robert Foarde and Elezabeth Addams which is subscribed in this Register in the yeare Anno Dni 1695, July 4th, He the said Robert Foarde was marred in ye 19 yeare of his age and she the said Elezabeth Addams was marred to Robert Foarde in the 22d yeare of her age written per me October 8th 1702.   Robertus Foarde.

(Signature at foot), Robertus Foarde, gent.

Page 21.   Original paging 13.
Two entries have been erased.

1662.

Jan. 21 (?)   Johes Duncombe Mag. Art. institut. & inductus ad presentacionem Joh'is Strode de Knighton gen. p. hac vice ver. & indubitat. patron.
Articulos legit et ijsdem subscripsit & ijsdem volens assensū & consensū p'buit in p'sentia nrū. quorū. noia. subscribuntr

1662.

22 Feb.   Arthur Newman sonne of Peter Newman was baptised (crossed through).
10 March.   Williā. Master buryed.
16   „   Joseph Ewyns of Evershott and Jane Tuck of Thornford, married.

1663.

9 June.   Eliz. daughter of Edw. Harris bapt.
[Torn]   ——— son of John Luckis baptised.
[Torn]   ——— Wills and Margaret Allerd marryed.
[Torn]   ——iam son of Peter Newman baptised.

---

* Another handwriting and probably not 1660.
† See note on page 16.

2

1664.

[Torn]	Samuel (?) son of Charles Panter buried.
— May.	Samuel son of Charles Panter buried.
[Torn]	Eliz. daughter of John Coxe bapt.
17 July.	Will. son of Samuel Master bapt.
19 Jan.	Joseph son of Geo. Master bapt.

1665.

15 May.	Edward son of Charles Panter of Knighton bapt.
24 „	William son of James Gooldryng bapt.
16 June.	William son of James Gooldryng buried.
1 Nov.	Mary daughter of Luke Thresher, bapt.
29 „	John son of Peter Newman bapt.
28 Jan.	Eliz. daughter of Ralph Pope of Yetminster bapt.

Page 22.

1666.

15 Jan.	Anne daughter of Geo. Master bapt.
12 March.	Susan Dowle of Knighton buryed.

1667.

8 April.	George son of John Somerset bapt.
6 Aug.	Geo. son of John Somersett *alias* Coxe bur.
4 Jan.	William Bartlett and Hester Young married.
16 Feb.	Robert son of Charles Panter bapt.

1668.

No entries.

1669.

29 March.	Edward son of Robert [torn]
12 April.	Josuah son of Josuah [torn, ? Ryall]
16 June.	Susanna daughter of Peter Newman bapt.
27 Dec.	Thomas Pomeroy and Susan Harris married.

1670.

No entries.

1671.

17 July.	John White of Bemister and Elizabeth Masters married.
15 Oct.	Robert sonne of Robert Patten baptised.
7 Nov.	Joane daughter of Trustrum Combe baptised.
16 „	Margery wife of Joshuah Ryall, buried.
19 Dec.	Joshuah son of Joshuah Ryall buried.
24 „	Luke Thesher buried.
27 Feb.	Joane daughter of George Masters buried.

Page 23. Original paging 16 (?). [Several pages missing.]

1696.

5 July.	Gertrude daughter of William and Gertrude Wiffen of Leigh, bapt.
6 Oct.	Thomas sonn of Thomas and Elizabeth Squire, bapt.
16 Dec.	Ellenor Webber, widdow, buried.
14 Feb.	Mary daughter of John and Mary Munden, bapt.
14 ,,	James Goldring, Clerke, buried.
14 March.	Elizabeth daughter of William and Julian Abbott bapt.
14 ,,	James son of William and Mary Hunt, bapt.
18 ,,	Charles Panter of Knighton, bur.

1697.

6 April.	Christian daughter of Joseph and Sarah Perrott, bapt.
20 ,,	Tristram Combe, bur.
12 Oct.	Richard sonn of Samuel and Christian Noak bapt.
28 Nov.	Sarah daughter of Josua and Sarah Ryall, bapt.
14 Dec.	Edward Harris Sr., of Knighton, bur.
2 Jan.	Richard sonn of Richard and Hannah Ryall of Ryme, bur.
21 March.	Samuel Pomeroy of Knighton, buried.

1698.

[Torn] 8 June.	Edward Harris of Knighton and Sarah Justins of Leigh marr.
10 June.	[torn] Potten and Mary Symms, marr.
[Torn] Aug.	[torn] ry daughter of Robert and Mary Shephard, bapt.
[Torn] Aug.	Widdow Harris of Knighton, bur.
[Torn] Nov.	Sarah daughter of Josua and Sarah Ryall, bur.
29 Jan.	Thomas Squire, buried.

1699.

11 April.	Susanna daughter of Alice Goldring, bur.
27 ,,	Samuel Noak of Knighton was buried at Foke.
2 May.	Charity daughter of Edward and Sarah Harris bapt.
2 ,,	Robert Shephard, bur.
15 July.	Mary Burrowes, widdow, bur.
24 Sept.	Charity daughter of Edward and Sarah Harris, bur.
29 Oct.	Robert Masters of Tybbles, bur.
30 ,,	Edward sonn of James and Mary Potten, bapt.

1700.

7 April.	James sonn of Joshua and Sarah Ryall, bapt.
26 ,,	Alice Goldring, widdow, bur.
26 ,,	George sonn of Edward and Sarah Harris, bapt.
5 July.	Robert Churchhouse bur.
3 Jan.	Grace Masters of Tybbals in ye parish of Knighton, bur.

30 March. Susanna daughter of Will. and Joan Dowle, bapt.
13 June.   Susanna wife of Joseph Perrott of Knighton, bur.
13   ,,   Benjamin and Elleanor son and daughter of Joseph
           Perrott, bapt.
16   ,,   Ellenor daughter of Joseph Perrott, buried.
10 Sept.   Widdow Thresher of Knighton, bur.
16   ,,   James sonn of James and Mary Patten, bapt.
23   ,,   Susanna daughter of Edward and Sarah Harris, bapt.

Page 24.

23 Nov.*   Thomas son of Thomas and Susanne Gennins of [? Rime]
           baptised.
30   ,,   Thomas son of Thomas and Susanna Gennings buried.
 1 Jan.   Mary daughter of William and Julian Abbott, bapt.
11   ,,   James sonn of Joshua and Sarah Ryall, bur.

1702.

19 Dec.   Thomas Masters, buryed.
20   ,,   Ann daughter of Richard Guyer and Deborah his wife
           baptised.
10 Feb.   Edward Harris, son of Edward, baptised.
23   ,,   Edward Harris, son of Edward, buried.
15 March. Ann Guyer, buried.

Signatures of Henry Emery, Rector.

John Adams   }
Edward Harris } Churchwardens.

1703.

 8 Aug.   William the spurious child of Elizabeth Masters was baptised.
28 Dec.   Thomas the son of John and Eleanor Vivian was baptised.
 3 March. Richard the son of Edward and Sa [torn†] ris was baptised.
20 June.‡ Joanna daughter of Richᵈ· and Deborah Guyer was baptised.

Signature of Hen. Emery, Rector.

1704.

20 June.   Joanna daughter of Richᵈ· and Deborah Guyer was baptised.
26 Sept.   Jane ye daughter of Susannah Newman, ye father unknown,
           bapt.
26   ,,   Joanna ye daughter of Ricd. Guyer was buried.
28   ,,   John son of John and Ann Munden was baptised.
27 Dec.   John Buckland and Mary Glide were married.
10 Jan.   William ye son of Joshua and Sarah Ryall was baptised.

-----

* This entry almost illegible.

† Probably Sarah Harris.

‡ This entry is crossed out and appears in the following year.

1705.

18 Aug.	John Addams the sone of John Addams buryed.
30 July.	John the sone of John Buckland and Mary his wife, baptised and John William Hugh Cross baptised at the same tyme.
17 Sept.	John the son of Richard and Deborah Guyer was bapt.
20 Nov.	John ye son of Richard Guyer was buried.
27 Dec.	Sarah ye daughter of Edward and Sarah Harris was bapt.
17 Jan.	Elizabeth daughter of James and Mary Patten was bapt.
27 Feb.	Robert Patten was buried.

Signature of Hen. Emery, Rector.

1706.

7 May.	Katharine Comb widdow was buried.
8 Nov.	Jonathan Parrott was buried.
20 Dec.	*Ann Patten was buried.
2 March.	Elizabeth daughter of John and Elizabeth Woollridge bapt.

1707.

4 May.	Elizabeth daughter of John and Elizabeth Woollridge buried.
18 May.	Joshua Ryal was buried.
29 June.	Joseph Parrott was buried.

Page 25. Original paging 22.

1725.

| 26 March. | Mary Masters was buried and affidavit made. |

8 April 1725.

Signatures of Ric. Bingham.
Wm. Freke.

25 April.	William Masters was buried. Aff. made 28 Apl.
31 May.	Johanna Abbott was buried. Aff. made 6 June.
9 July.	Mary daughter of William and Elizabeth Masters bapt.
22 Sept.	Mary Ailesbury was buried. No aff.
17 Jan.	Samuel son of Edward and Martha Noak was bapt.
9 Feb.	John Summerset was buried. Aff. made 22 Feb.

21 April 1726. Allowed by us,

Ric. Bingham.
Wm. Freke.

1726.

2 June.	John Apthye was buried. Aff. made 3 June.
1 Oct.	Julian Abbot was buried. Aff. made 9 Oct.
5 „	William son of John and Ruth Toop was bapt.

* Mary crossed out.

8 March.	Orlando Napper and Mellicent Payn were married.
18 „	Hannah Ryal was buried. Aff. made 19 March.

Allowed by us, April ye 11, 1727.

Ric. Bingham.
Wm. Freke.

1727.

14 Sept.	John Burrows was buried. Aff. made 25 Sept.
11 March.	Robert son of John and Ruth Toop was bapt.

1728.

26 May.	William Masters son of William and Elizabeth was bapt.
19 July.	Benjamin son of James and Elizabeth Patten was bapt.
28 „	Benjamin Patten was buried. Aff. made 5 Aug.
22 Dec.	Margaret daughter of John and Ann Woolridge was bapt.
5 Jan.	Edward Hayward and Mary Lane were married.
19 „	Luke Thresher was buried. Aff. made 28 Jan.
2 Feb.	John Woollridge was buried. Aff. made the same evening.
9 „	Margaret Woolridge was buried. Aff. made 11 March.

April 17th, 1729. Allowed by us,

Ric. Bingham.
J. H. Wicksted.

Page 26.

1729.

30 April.	Mary Abbott was buried. Aff. made 5 May.
24 July.	John Harris was buried. Aff. made 28 July.
3 Aug.	Anthony Mandefeild and Ann Moor were married.
21 Sept.	John Summersett was buried. Aff. made 29 Sept.
10 Dec.	Mary wife John Davison buried. Aff. made 14 Dec.
11 Jan.	Ann Brown was buried. Aff. made 19 Jan.
9 Feb.	Charles son of Robt. and Mary Cook was bapt.
22 „	Ann Woollridge was buried. Aff made 1 March.
21 March.	Richard son of Charles and Elizabeth Noak was bapt.

Allowed by us. April ye 17th, 1730.

Ric. Bingham.
Wm. Freke.

1730.

14 Sept.	Elizabeth daughter of John and Mary Baker was bapt.
24 „	Elizabeth Baker was buried. Aff. made 27 Sept.
10 Oct.	Thomas son of John and Ruth Toup was bapt.
24 Jan.	George Harris was buried. Aff. made 29 Jan.
16 Feb.	John son of James and Elizabeth Patten was bapt.

Allowed by us, 29 April 1731.

(No signatures.)

1731.

20 June.	James Patten was buried. Aff. made 23 June.
9 July.	John Patten was buried. Aff. made 10 July.
30 Aug.	Elizabeth daughter of John and Mary Baker was bapt.
30 Oct.	William Masters was buried. Aff. made the same day.
21 Dec.	Charles son of Charles and Elizabeth Noak was bapt.
30 Jan.	Elizabeth Cox was buried. Aff. made 5 Feb.

Signature of Hen. Embris, Rector.

17 April, 1732. Allowed by us,
Ric. Bingham.
Wm. Freke.

1732.

1 June.	Elizabeth daughter of Robert and Mary Cook was bapt.
27 ,,	Joan Jacob was buried. Aff. made 1 July.
17 July.	John Thresher of Netherbury and Christian Woolridge of Beerhacket were married.
21 Aug.	John the son of Edward and Martha Noak was bapt.
24 Sept.	Ann Buckland was buried. Aff. made 26 Sept.
29 Oct.	Elizabeth daughter of John and Ruth Toup was bapt.
14 Nov.	Robert Toup was buried. Aff. made 15 Nov.
31 Jan.	Mary daughter of Robert and Joan Buckland was bapt.

5 April, 1733. Allowed by us,
Ric. Bingham.
Wm. Freke.

Page 27. Original paging 23.

1733.

17 May.	Richard Noak was buried. Aff. made 23 May.
10 June.	George Dunham and Sarah Tuck were married.
19 Feb.	Thomas Abbott was buried. Aff. made 24 Feb.
20 March.	Richard son of Charles and Elizabeth Noak was bapt.

25 April, 1724. Allowed by us,
Ric. Bingham.
Wm. Freke.

1734.

29 Aug.	George and Fanny Harris were buried. Aff. made 31 Aug.
25 Nov.	Charles Noak was buried. Aff. made 1 Dec.
1 Dec.	Richard Summerset was buried. Aff. made 9 Dec.
19 March.	John the son of Robert and Sarah Brown was bapt.

17 April, 1735. Allowed by us,
Ric. Bingham.
Wm. Freke.

1735.

14 May.   John the son of Robert and Joan Buckland was bapt.
14 Sept.   James Summersett was buried. Aff. made 21 Sept.
30 Dec.   Christian the daughter of Charles and Elizabeth Noak was bapt.

      6 May, 1736. Allowed by us,
          Thos. Medlycott.
          Tho. Freke.

1736.

4 Aug.   Ann the daughter of Winsor and Katharine Guyer was bapt.
26 April.   Thomas Moor and Rebeccha Willmott were married.
3 Oct.   Robert Patten was buried. Aff. made same day.
16 Dec.   Hannah Baker was buried. Aff. made 20 Dec.
18 Feb.   Robert the son of John and Ruth Toup was bapt.

1737.

6 April.   George Harris was buried. Aff. made 9 April.

      21 April, 1737. Allowed by us,
      (No signatures.)

17 July.   Robert Oliver was buried.
18 Sept.   George Harris was buried.
23 Jan.   John Woolridge was buried. Aff. made 24 Jan.

         Signature of Henry Embris.

      13 April, 1738. Allowed by us,
          Wm. Freke.
          Tho. Freke.

1738.

10 Nov.   William Toop was buried. Aff. made 12 Dec.
5 Dec.   Mary daughter of Winsor and Katharine Guyer was bapt.
4 May.   Robert Holly and Ann Andrews were married.

1739.

30 March.   Windsor Guyer was buried. Aff. made 8 April.
24 April.   Sarah Harris was buried. Aff. made 4 May.

      5 May, 1739. Allowed by us,
          Wm. Freke.
          Tho. Freke.

14 May.   Edward Harris of Beerhagard and Sarah Dyke were married.
17 May.   Elizabeth Cake was buried. Aff. made 18 May.

      Page 28.

21 May.   William Cake was buried. Aff. made 21 May.
12 June.   Mary the daughter of John and Ruth Toup was bapt.
25   „   William Masters was buried. Aff. made 26 June.
29 Oct.   William son of Thomas and Hannah Masters was bapt.

5 Nov. Priscilla Masters was buried. Aff. was made 11 Nov.
27 Dec. Charles Harvey and Jemima Harris were married.

   17 April, 1740. Allowed by us,
    Tho. Medlycott.
    Tho. Freke.

1740.

30 June. Richard son of Charles and Jemima Harris was bapt.
14 July. Mary Harris was buried. Aff. made 18 July.

   9 April, 1741. Allowed by us,
    Wm. Freke.
Henry Embris, Rector.—Tho. Freke.

1741.

21 April. Elizabeth Oliver was buried. Aff. made 26 April.
9 Aug. Mary daughter of Thomas and Hannah Masters was bapt.
24 „ Sarah Masters was buried. Aff. made 28 Aug.

1742.

14 Feb. George Buckland and Ann Harman were married.
8 March. Richard Ryal was buried. Aff. made. Was buried in woollen.

1743.

27 March. Hugh the son of Hugh and Mary Granger was bapt.
23 April. Hugh Granger was buried.
24 „ Robert son of Thomas and Melior Pidle was bapt.
1 May. William son of John and Ruth Toup was buried.

1744.

11 March. Robert son of Hugh and Mary Granger bapt.
10 March. William son of John and Ruth Toup was bapt.
8 July. Joan Cozins was buried in woollen only.
— Aug. William Masters was buried in woollen only.
24 8ber. Eliz. Foard was buried in woollen only.
*26 July. 1773. Richard Noake was buried in woollen only.
*6 Feb. 1774. John Darby was buried in woollen only.
*24 Feb. 1774. John Gould was buried in woollen only.

1745.

4 Aug. Wm. son of Thos. & Melior Piddle was bapt.
3 7ber. Hugh son of Hugh and Mary Granger bapt.
15 Oct. Edward Noake of Knighton was buried in woollen only.

1746.
No entries.

† 1773.

22 Apl. Saml. son of John & Mary Darby bapt.

---

 * Out of place here, but so in Register.
 † Out of place.

VOLUME II.

Burials.

Page 1.

1773.

26 July.   Richard Noake was buried in woollen only.

1774.

8 Feb.   John Darby was buried in woollen only.
24 Feb.   John Gould was buried in woollen only.

1775.

19 Dec.   Edward Noake was buried in woollen only.

1777.

3 Feb.   Elizabeth Harris was buried in woollen only.
9 Oct.   Mary Noake was buried in woollen only.
2 Nov.   Edward Noake was buried in woollen only.

1778.

29 May.   Joseph King was buried in woollen only.

1779.

18 Feb.   John Noake was buried in woollen only. Aff. made 22nd.

1782.

6 March.   Betty Masters was buried in woollen only.
16 Oct.   Thomas Masters was buried in woollen only.
8 Dec.   William Masters was buried in woollen only.

1783.

23 Feb.   Samuel Masters was buried in woollen only.
14 May.   John Toop was buried in woollen only.

1784.

23 June.   Jane Russel Munden was buried in woollen only.   Paid.

1785.

19 June.   Samuel Noake, pauper, discharged by the Act.

1786.

21 May.   Judith Hicks a pauper.
2 July.   Sarah daughter of Samuel and Sarah Masters.   Paid.

1789.

10 Nov.   John Granger, pauper, was buried.   Paid.

1791.

27 June.   James Cake was buried.   Paid.
3 Nov.   Mary Gould was buried.

1792.

13 Nov.   Mary Notley was buried.

Page 2.

1794.

11 Jan.   Elizabeth Toop was buried.
6 May.   Charles Gould was buried.

1796.

9 Jan.   John son of Richard and Charlotte Gould was buried.

1797.

25 May.   Ann daughter of Simon and Margary Granger was buried.
8 August.   William son of John and Betty Andrews was buried.

1798.

27 May.   Jenny daughter of Simon and Margary Granger was buried.
21 Dec.   Susannah Munden was buried.

1799.

24 Nov.   Mary Masters wife of Robert Masters was buried.

1800.

1 July.   Jane daughter of Richard and Charlotte Gould was buried.
3 Dec.   Elizabeth daughter of Richard and Charlotte Gould was buried.

1801.

11 Jan.   Thomas son of Robert and Mary Masters was buried.

1802.

26 July.   George Toop was buried.

Page 3.

7 Nov.   Hannah Masters was buried.

1803.

20 Jan.   Thomas Masters was buried.

1804.

18 Nov.   Joseph son of Edward and Susannah Taylor was buried.

1805.

12 May.   Rachel daughter of Robert and Betty Masters was buried.

1806.

3 Nov.   Susannah daughter of Robert and Betty Masters was buried.

1810.

13 May.   Elizabeth Masters was buried.

1812.

9 March.   William son of Simon and Margary Granger was buried.

Baptisms.

Page 33.

1773.

22 April.   Samuel son of John and Mary Darby, baptised.

1775.

16 June.   Christian daughter of Richard and Elizabeth Harris, bap.
27 Nov.   Edward son of Samuel and Agnes Noake, baptiz'd.
4 Dec.   Betty daughter of Thomas and Mary Axtence, bap.

1776.

26 May.   Mary Lamess daughter of Thos. and Elizabeth Samson, bap.

1777.

4 May.   Edward son of Samuel and Agnes Noake, bapt^{d}.
25 May.   John son of Simon and Margery Granger, bapt^{d}.
8 June.   Betty daughter of Thos. and Elizabeth Samnson, bapt^{d}.

1778.

25 April.   Joseph and Benjamin sons of Thomas and Elizabeth King, bap.
19 Nov.   Thomas son of Thos. and Elizabeth Samson, bap.
30 Nov.   George son of Simon and Margery Granger, bap.

1779.

None.

1780.

8 May.   Ann daughter of Simon and Margery Granger, bap.

1781.

20 April.	Mary daughter of Henry and Hannah Gill, baptized.
21 August.	William son of James and Rachel Cake, baptized.
20 Sept.	Ann daughter of Robert and Mary Masters, baptized.
30 Sept.	Ann daughter of Thos. and Elizabeth Samson, baptized.

Page 34.

1782.

14 April.	Ann daughter of Richard and Susannah Green, baptized.
1 Sept.	Thos son of Simon and Margery Granger, baptized.
13 Nov.	John Maber son of John and Jane Munden, baptized.

1783.

16 Feb.	Jane base born daughter of Mary Squib, baptized.
12 March.	Elizabeth daughter of Henry and Hannah Gill, baptized.
28 Dec.	Mary daughter of James and Rachel Cake, baptized. Born 24 Dec. 1783.

1784.

12 March.	Mary daughter of Robert and Mary Masters, baptized. Born 16 Jan. 1784.
18 March.	Martha daughter of Thomas and Elizabeth Samson, bapt., born 8 March 1784.
30 May.	Susannah daughter of Richard and Susannah Green, baptized, born 30 April 1784. Paid.

1785.

7 August.	Sarah daughter of Samuel and Sarah Masters.
2 Oct.	John son of Henry and Hannah Gill. Paid.

1786.

1 Jan.	Wm and James sons of Simon and Margery Granger.
25 April.	William son of John and Jane Munden.

Page 35.

30 April.	James son of John and Elizabeth Toop. Paid.
25 Dec.	Thomas son of Edward and Susannah Taylor.

1787.

21 Jan.	Elizabeth daughter of James and Rachael Cake. Paid.

1788.

17 Jan.	Charlotte and George daughter and son of George and Sarah Ryall.
3 Feb.	Elizabeth daughter of Robert and Mary Masters.
3 Feb.	John son of John and Elizabeth Toop.
23 March.	Henry son of Simon and Margery Granger. Paid.

1789.

29 March.	John son of James and Rachael Cake.
9 Aug.	John base born son of Eleanor Hoskins.
20 Sept.	Margaret daughter of Edward and Susannah Taylor.
4 Oct.	Sarah daughter of Samuel and Sarah Masters. Paid.

1790.

23 May.	Mary daughter of Simon and Margery Granger.
1 August.	Ruth daughter of Robert and Mary Masters.
25 Dec.	Ann Miles daughter of John and Elizabeth Toop. Paid.

1791.

27 June.	Richard son of James and Rachael Cake.
17 July.	Mary daughter of William and Jane Notley.
23 Oct.	John son of Joseph and Mary Andrews was baptized.
23 Oct.	Betty daughter of John and Betty Andrews was baptized.

1792.

12 Feb.	William son of Edward and Susannah Taylor was baptized.
1 July.	Samuel son of Samuel and Sarah Master was baptized.
14 Oct.	Betty daughter of Simon and Marjary Granger was baptized.

1793.

20 Jan.	Robert son of Robert and Mary Masters was baptized.
21 March.	Ruth daughter of John and Betty Toop was baptized.
35 Aug.	Mary daughter of John and Betty Andrews was baptized.
25 Aug.	Elizabeth daughter of Thomas & Sarah Downton was baptized.

1794.

23 March.	Martha daughter of Richard and Rachel Noake was christened.
8 June.	John son of Richard and Charlotte Gould was baptized.
29 June.	William son of John and Betty Andrews was christened.

1795.

1 March.	Joseph son of Edward and Susannah Taylor was baptised.

Page 37.

25 Dec.	Mary daughter of Richard and Charlotte Gould was baptised.

1796.

3 March.	Richard son of Richard and Rachael Noake was christened.
22 May.	John son of Robert and Mary Masters was baptised.
19 June.	Jenny daughter of Simon and Margary Granger was christened.
19 June.	William son of John and Elizabeth Toop was baptised.
14 Sept.	John and Elizabeth son and daughter of William and Jane Notley were christened.

1797.

26 March. Elizabeth daughter of Richard and Charlotte Gould was baptized.
10 Sept. Ann daughter of Simon and Margary Granger was baptized.
8 Oct. Joseph son of John and Betty Andrews was baptized.

1798.

19 August. John base-born son of Eleanora Hoskins was baptized.

1799.

7 April. Jane daughter of Richard and Charlotte Gould was baptized.
8 Sept. Thomas son of John and Betty Toop was baptized.

1800.

3 Dec. Elizabeth daughter of Richard and Charlotte Gould was christened.

Page 38.

1801.

4 Jan. Rachel daughter of Richard and Rachel Noake was christened.
20 Sept. Hannah daughter of Robert and Betty Masters was christened.

1802.

16 May. Betty daughter of Henry and Elizabeth Priddle was christened.
1 June. Frances daughter of James and Elizabeth Cake was christened.

1803.

29 May. George son of John and Mary Saunders was baptized.
3 July. Thomas son of Robert and Betty Masters was christened.
25 Sept. John son of Henry and Elizabeth Priddle was christened.

1804.

25 Dec. Sarah daughter of James and Elizabeth Cake was christened.

1805.

7 April. George base-born son of Ann Masters was christened.
14 April. Samuel son of Henry and Elizabeth Priddle was baptized.
5 May. Susannah daughter of Robert and Betty Masters was baptized.

1806.

17 August. Ann daughter of Henry and Elizabeth Priddle was christened.

Page 39.

1807.

22 March. Ann daughter of James and Ann Crocker was christened.

1808.

17 April. William son of Robert and Betty Masters was baptized.

23 July. James son of Robert & Betty Masters.

1810.

6 May. Jane daughter of Jacob and Martha Osmond was baptized.

27 May. Henry and Alfred sons of Henry and Elizabeth Priddle were baptized.

29 July. John son of Robert and Mary Strange of Cerne Abbas was baptized.

23 Sept. John son of Samuel Rendall was baptized.

1811.

13 Oct. Ann daughter of Jacob and Martha Osmond was baptized.

1812.

10 May. Harriett daughter of Thomas and Elizabeth Taylor was baptized.

17 May. Caroline daughter of Mary Snook was baptized, base born.

Page 55.

Memorandum. 1798. 29 August. A copy from the Register sent to Sherborne Visitation.

Memorandum. 1799. 14 August. A copy from the Register sent to Sherborne Visitation.

Memorandum. 1806. 12 August. A copy from the Register to this time sent to Sherborne.

Memorandum. 1807. 18 August. A copy of the Register to this time sent to Sherborne.

Memorandum. 1808. 16 August. A copy of the Register to this time sent to Sherborne.

Memorandum. 1810. 14 August. A copy of the Register sent to Sherborne.

Memorandum. 1811. 25 June. A copy of the Register sent to Sherborne.

Memorandum. 1812. 18 August. A copy of the Register sent to Sherborne.

Memorandum. 1313. 27 July. A copy of the Register sent to Sherborne.

VOLUME III.

— —

Marriages, 1757=1812.

1757.　6 June.　Thomas Toop of this parish and Mary Sherring of Bradford Abbas, by Banns, by Robert Sampson, Rector. Witnesses, E. Hosey, junr., Thomas Masters.

1759.　5 Feb.　John Sherring of Bradford Abbas and Mary Toop of this parish, by Banns, by Edward Cheselden, Officiating Minister. Witnesses, E. Hosey, junr., Thomas Masters.

1759.　19 Nov.　John Beaton a sojourner in this parish and Elizabeth Toop of this parish, by Banns, by Robert Sampson, Rector. Witnesses, E. Hosey, junr., Thomas Masters.

1761.　9 April.　John Noake of Knighton in this parish and Mary Barnet of Sherborne, by License, by Robert Sampson, Rector. Witnesses, Charles Noake, Richard Noake.

1761.　13 April.　Thomas Loader of this parish and Elizabeth Riddle a sojourner in Lillington, by Banns, by Robert Sampson, Rector. Witnesses, John Loader, Joseph Loader.

1762.　5 Jan.　Richard Goldring and Jone Piddle both of this parish, by Banns, by Robert Sampson, Rector. Witnesses, Thomas Masters, William Coombes.

1762.　18 May.　Samuel Noake of Knighton and Agnes Coward of Bradford, by Banns, by J. Topham, Off. Min. Witnesses, Thomas Masters, Christian Long.

1762.　9 Aug.　John Toop and Elizabeth Wakeley, both of this parish, by Banns, by Robert Sampson, Rector. Witnesses, Thomas Melmoth, Hannah Masters.

1762.　6 Dec.　Stephen Abbot and Love Gould, both of this parish, by Banns, by Robert Sampson, Rector. Witnesses not named.

1763.　7 April.　Adam Abbot and Betty Bartlet, both of this parish, by Banns, by Robert Sampson, Rector. Witnesses, Thomas Masters, Ed. Harris.

1763.　4 July.　Stephen Abbot of this parish and Sarah Linnard of Melbury Osmond, by License, by Robert Sampson, Rector. Witnesses, Richard Noake, Thomas Masters.

3

1765. 21. Oct. William Bird of this parish and Susanna Tomkyns of Yetminster, by License, by Robert Sampson, Rector. Witnesses, John Smith, Thomas Masters.

(No date given.) Richard Harris of Yetminster and Betty Spurle of this parish, by Banns, by Robert Sampson, Rector. Witnesses John Lill, Thomas Masters.

1770. 22 Nov. Thomas Moor of Thornford and Lare (*sic*) Mead of this parish, by Banns, by Robert Sampson, Rector. Witnesses, Thomas Masters, Ann Granger.

1771. 5 Jan. William Toop of this parish and Betty Gill of Over Compton, by Banns, by Robert Sampson, Rector. Witnesses, Thomas Masters, Henry Gill.

1771. 23 Dec. James Hunt and Sarah Crocker both of this parish, by Banns, by Robert Sampson, Rector. Witnesses, Thomas Masters, Grace Jeanes.

1773. 29 April. Robert Cox of Shenton Magna, co. Dorset, and Sarah Mabar, of Knighton in this parish, by License, by Robert Sampson, Rector. Witnesses, George Russell, Thomas Masters.

1775. 3 July. · Thomas Axtence and Mary Hannam both of this parish, by Banns, by Robert Sampson, Rector. Witnesses, Thomas Masters, Simon Granger.

1775. 5 Nov. Benjamin Warren and Betty Toop, both of this parish, by Banns, by Robert Sampson, Rector. Witnesses, Thomas Masters, Thomas Masters, jun.

1776. 4 July. Simon Granger of this parish and Margery Dunning of Buckland, by License, by Robert Sampson, Rector. Witnesses, Richard Chapman, Robert Duning.

1777. 9 Mch. Joseph Courtney and Hannah Masters, both of this parish, by Banns, by Robert Sampson, Rector. Witnesses, Thomas Axtens, Sarah Masters.

1777. 14 Aug. Richard Harris and Mary Gould, both of this parish, by Banns, by Robert Sampson, Rector. Witnesses, Thomas Masters, Joseph Coodney.

1779. 12 July. Thomas Masters, jun., and Mary Hodges Downton, both of this parish, by Banns, by Robert Sampson, Rector. Witnesses, Samuel Masters, Betty Downton, junr.

1779. 1 Dec. Daniel Besant of Yeatminster, and Elizabeth Mitchell of Knighton in this parish, by License, by Robert Sampson, Rector. Witnesses, George Bryer, Gertrude Munden.

1780. 21 Mch. George Johnson of Sanford Orcas and Frances Watts, widow, of this parish, by Banns, by John Munden, Curate. Witnesses, Samuel Bullen, Thomas Masters.

1780. 30 May. Robert Masters and Mary Paully both of this parish, by Banns, by John Munden, Curate. Witnesses, Joseph Courtney, Thomas Masters.

1781. 16 Aug. Joseph Courtney and Gertrude Munden, both of this parish, by License, by Robert Sampson, Rector. One witness, Susanna Spencer.

1783. 3. 10. 17. Aug. *Banns only.* James Hunt of Thornford and Mary Squeb *otherwise* Skeeb of Knighton in this parish, published 3, 10 and 17 August, 1783.

1785. 16 Nov. Joseph Chisman of Yetminster and Esther Scott, spinster, of this parish, by Banns, by John Munden, Rector. Witnesses, Simon Granger, John Toop.

1786. 16 Oct. Joseph Willmington of this parish and Mary Holloway of Barwick, by Banns, by John Munden, Rector. Witnesses, Juletter Sherring, Jane Woollmington.

1787. 20 Feb. John Higgins of this parish, and Mary Brooke of Trent, spinster, by License, by John Munden, Rector. Witnesses, Elizabeth Sherring, Juletter Sherring.

1793. 10 April. Richard Gould and Charlotte Giles, both of this parish, by Banns, by Robert Harbin, Curate. Witnesses, Simon Granger, Mary Masters.

1793 8 May. Richard Noake and Rachel Cake, both of this parish, by Banns, by Robert Harbin, Curate. Witnesses, Simon Granger, Jemima Trim.

1795. 1 July. George Trim of this parish and Sarah Jefferey, of Yetminster, by Banns, by Robert Harbin, Curate. Witnesses, Thomas Jeffery, Alios Sansom.

1796. 22 June. Matthew Cox of Leigh and Elizabeth Sansom (or Samson) of this parish, by Banns, by Robert Harbin, Curate. Witnesses, Thomas Salisbury, Elizabeth Cox.

180c. 11 Mch. Robert Masters of this parish and Elizabeth Tollevill of Thornford, spinster, by Banns, by Robert Harbin, Curate. Witnesses, Simon Granger, Charles Notley.

1801. 23 June. James Cake and Elizabeth Saunders, both of this parish, by Banns, by Robert Harbin, Curate. Witnesses, Simon Granger, Richard Noake.

1802. 30 Aug. Daniel Hunt of Leigh and Elizabeth Priddle, sojourner in this parish, by Banns, by Robert Harbin, Curate. Witnesses, Henry Priddle, Elizabeth Cake.

1803. 11 April. George Snook, sojourner, and Mary Cake, of this parish, by Banns, by Robert Harbin, Curate. Witnesses, Elizabeth Toop, Simon Granger.

1806. 14 May.   Charles Notley of Dewlish and Elizabeth Toop of this parish, by Banns, by Robert Harbin, Curate. Witnesses, Thomas Toop, Sarah Elsen (?)

1809. 24 Aug.   Jacob Osment and Martha Toop, both of this parish, by Banns, by William Munden, Curate. Witnesses, George Newman, Hester Hembury.

1810. 3 Feb.   Robert Strange of Cerne Abbas and Mary Toop of this parish, by License, by William Munden, Curate. Witnesses, Richard Buckland, Elizabeth Strange.

1811. 23 April.   Thomas Taylor and Elizabeth Masters, both of this parish, by Banns, by Thomas Bellamy, Curate. Witnesses, John Toop, Sara Masters.

1812. 17 April.   William Sartin and Ruth Toop, both of this parish, by Banns, by Thomas Bellamy, Curate. Witnesses, John Toop, Robert Masters.

Index Nominum.

COMPILED BY SIDNEY MADGE, ESQ., F.R.H.S.

[———— Edward 18; Robert 18.]

Abbott, Adam 33; Eliz. 19; Joan 21; Jul. 19, 20, 21 ; Mary, 20, 22 : Steph. 35*; Thos. 23; Wm 19, 20.

Adams (Addams), Eliz., 16, 17*; John 20, 21.*

Ailesbury, Mary 21.

Allerd, Margaret 17.

Allwood (Allwod), Jas. 15 ; John 15*; Mary 15.

Andrews (Androwes), Ann 24; Betty 27, 30*, 31; John 27, 30*, 31 ; Jos. 30; Mary 30*; Wm. 3, 4*, 27, 30, vi.

Apthye, John 21.

Atkins (see Hatkins).

Axtence, Thos. 34* (see also Oxtence).

Baker, Eliz. 22, 23 ; Hann. 24; John 22, 23; Mary 22, 23.

Barnard, Emm. 6.

Barnet, Mary 33.

Bartlet (Bartlett), Alex. 13 ; Betty 33 ; Wm. 18.

Bauller (Bauler, Bavller, Bawller), Agnes 2; Alice 8; Ann 7, 11, 12 ; Basil 9; Bennett 3, 7,* 8,* 9, 12 ; Chris. 8; Edith 3; Elean. 8; Eliz. 6, 10; Emm. 7; Grace, 8, 14 ; Joan 2, 10; John 1*, 2*, 3*, 7*, 8*, 9, 10*, 14 ; Martha 7, 11; Ric. 7; Rob. 1, 9; Thos. 3; Wm. 1, 2, 10, 15*.

Bearlye, Ric. 6.

Beaton, John 33.

Bellamy, Thos. 36*.

Besant, Dan. 34.

Bingham, Ric. 21*, 22*, 23*.

Bird, Wm. 34.

Bonfield, Thos. 5.

Braine (Brame), Wm. 14*.

Bristol, Earl of vi.

Brooke, Mary 35.

Brown (Browne), Ann 22; Hy. 11*, 12, vi.; Joan 11, 12; John 23; Lionel 13; Marg. 12; Rob. 23; Sar. 23; Thos. vi.

Bryer, Geo. 34.

Buckland, Ann 23; Geo. 25; Joan 23, 24; John 20, 21*, 24; Mary 21, 23; Rich. 36; Rob. 23, 24.

Bullen, Sam. 34.

Burnard, Arthur Chichester vii.

Burrows (Burrowes), John 22; Mary 19.

Burt (Birte), Joan 13; Jos.' 14; Rob. 13, 14.

Cake, Eliz. 24, 29, 31*, 35; Frances 31; Jas. 27, 29*, 30*, 31*, 35 ; John 30; Mary 29, 35; Rach. 29*, 30, 35; Ric. 30; Sar. 31; Wm. 24, 29.

Chamberlayne, Joan 9.

Chaplin, Ric. 2.

Chapman, Ric. 34.

Chappell, Agnes 6

Chedde, Ric. 10, 11'.

Cheselden, Edw. 33.

Chisman, Jos. 35.

Churchouse (Church house, Churche house, Churchowse, Churchuse), Abel 6, 9, 10, 11, 12, 13, 14, 15; Agnes 12*; Alice 6, 8; Anne, 2; Bridg. 2, 5; Cath. 12 ; Christopher 7, 12, 13; Dor. 7; Edith 12; Eliz. 11; Emma 5; Geo. 10; Grace 11, 15; Hy. 11, 14*; Jas. 11; Jane 15; Joan 7, 12;

Green, Ann 29; Ric. 29*; Sus. 29*.
Gregorie, Rog. 9.
Guppey, Const. 16*; Ric. 16.
Guye, Ralph 10.
Guyer, (Gwyer), Ann 20*, 24; Cath.
  24*; Deborah 20*, 21; Ellen 16;
  Joan 20*; John 21*; Mary 24;
  Ric. 16, 20*, 21*; Winsor 24*.

Hannam, Joan 3; Jn. 3; Mary 34.
Harbin, Robt. 35*, 36.
Harman, Ann, 25.
Harris (Harrys), Alice 2, 3, 10;
  Charity, 16, 19*; Chas. 25 Chris.
  28; Edw. 2, 3, 9, 16, 17*, 19*,
  20*, 21, 24, 33; Eliz. 17*, 26, 28;
  Fanny 23; Geo. 3, 8*, 19, 22, 23,
  24*; Jemima 25*; John 22;
  Louisa 9; Mary 25; Ric. 15, 20,
  25, 28, 34; Sar. 19*, 20*, 21*,
  24; Sus. 16, 18, 20; Widow 19;
  Wm. 8.
Harrison, Joan 9; Lionel 9.
Harvey, Chas. 25.
Hatkins, Han. 14; John 13*, 14.
Hawkins, John 1.
Hayward, Edw. 22.
Hearn, Eliz. 16.
Helyar, W. vii.; H. W. vii.
Hembury, Hester 36
Hicks, John 27.
Higgins, John 35.
Hill, Alice 6.
Himyngame, or Hinnygame, Amyas
  1*, vi.
Hodges, Anth. 6; Thos. 12*.
Holloway, Mary 35.
Holly, Rob. 24.
Hosey, E. 33*.
Hoskins, Elean. 30, 31; John 30, 31.
Hulett, Sus. 13.
Hull, Grace 8, 12; Thos. 8.
Hunt, Daniel 35; Jas. 19, 34, 35;
  Mary 19; Wm. 19.
Hutchings (Hutchins), Jasper 12*;
  Joan 12, 13; Mary 12.

Ingelbert, John 5.

Jacob, Joan 23.
Jeanes, Grace 34; John 5; Ric. 5.
Jeffery, Sar. 35; Thos. 35.
Jefferyes, Ric. vi.
Jeffris, Nich. 13, 14.
Jennings, see Gennings.
Johnson, Geo. 34.
Joyce, Ric. 5; Wm. 5.
Juskins, Sar. 19.
Juxon, Thos. 12.

Keat (Keate, Keytt), Elean. 4;
  Emm. 5; Hy. 5, 6; Joan 4; John
  4*, 5*; Phil. 4; Ric. 5.
Kente, Sim. 11; Thos. 11, 12.
Kimpe (Kymppe), Agnes 4; Phil.
  4.
King (Kinge), Benj. 28; Eliz. 28;
  John 8; Jos. 26, 28; Thos. 28.
Kingsmill (Kingsmell), Sir John 16;
  Thos. 16.

Lacy, Marg. 13.
Lambeth, Ann 13.
Lambert (Lamberte, Lambard,
  Lamberd), Ann. 11; Edw. 2, 13*,
  14*; Elean. 5, 14; Isab. 3; Joan
  5, 14; John 15; Marg. 3, 6, 10;
  Thos. 2, 3, 6.
Lane, Mary 22.
Latchmore, John 3.
Lester, Jas. 7.
Lewys, Ann vii.
Lill, John 34.
Linnard, Sarah 33.
Loader, John 33; Joseph 33; Thos.
  33.
Lodge, Joan 7, 9; Jas. 12.
Lokier, John 16.
Long, Christian 33.
Luckis, Arth. 13; Joan 13; John 14,
  17; Ric. 12; Wm. 12, 13*, 14.
Lye, John 11.

Mabar, Sarah 34.
Mandefield, Anth. 22.
Masson, Thos. 4.
Mast, Francis 13.

Index Locorum.

.

www.ingramcontent.com/pod-product-compliance
Lightning Source LLC
Chambersburg PA
CBHW021555270326
41931CB00009B/1224